CENTRAL AMERICANS IN MEXICO CITY:
UPROOTED AND SILENCED

Laura O'Dogherty

Hemispheric Migration Project
Center for Immigration Policy and Refugee Assistance
Georgetown University

ISBN: 0-924046-11-2

Cover photo: Pedro Valtierra/Cuartoscuro

To my godchildren

Laura Martinez and

Pablo Ortiz Monasterio

TABLE OF CONTENTS

LIST OF TABLES

Foreword

The Hemispheric Migration Project (HMP), sponsored by Georgetown University's Center for Immigration Policy and Refugee Assistance (CIPRA), funds research on refugees and labor migrants in Latin America and the Caribbean. The project's support of Latin American and Caribbean scholars has a twofold objective: to encourage the development of research on refugees and migration in countries of origin and to bring the results of this research to the attention of policy-makers in the sending, as well as receiving, countries. Since 1983, the HMP has commissioned and provided technical support for over 35 studies on the causes and consequences of population movements in the Western Hemisphere. On topics ranging from the repatriation process in Guatemala to skilled manpower loss in Jamaica, the HMP has provided information to policy-makers in the United States and throughout the hemisphere on a wide range of immigration and refugee-related problems. On the basis of this information, policies can be tailored to encourage the benefits of international migration and diminish its costs.

The Hemispheric Migration Project has been made possible by grants from the Bureau for Refugee Programs of the Department of State. Needless to say, we thank the Bureau and our colleagues, the scholars throughout Latin America and the Caribbean who have collaborated with us and without whom none of this work would be possible. We would also like to acknowledge the individuals who have helped bring this monograph to press: Charles Roberts, for translation; Patricia R. Pessar, Ph.D, Mary Ann Larkin, and Charles Becker for editing; Gerardo D. Berthin for production and artwork; and Asha Sekhri and Sherie Smith for production.

Harold Bradley, S.J.
Director, CIPRA

Patricia R. Pessar, Ph.D.
Research Director

"I was feeling a little out of it, and I began to think that, even if 5 million people paraded by me I wouldn't find a familiar face; and then I thought that it was worse than being in the desert....I began to remember the house, the old neighborhood, and the hamlets, and I told Anita I was wondering what her folks and little brother were up to at that moment...and she was about to speak and all of a sudden she broke into tears, sobbing like hell.... A wave of grief gripped her whole body and wouldn't let her breathe."

(Diary of a Migrant, Miguel Delibes)

INTRODUCTION

The displacement of thousands of Central Americans by repression, civil war, and massive violations of human rights and the severe economic deterioration are two dire consequences of the Central American social conflicts.* Since 1978, more than two million people from El Salvador, Nicaragua, Guatemala, and Honduras have abandoned their homes in search of security within their own countries, in neighboring countries, or in Mexico and the United States.

Mexico is the destination for tens of thousands of migrants. It is impossible to specify the exact magnitude of this migratory flow because of the undocumented status of the great majority. Some estimates indicate that from 17.5 to 22 percent of the migrants who have fled the region's conflicts have settled in different parts of Mexico. As of 1987, estimates of Central American migrants in Mexico ranged from 165,000 to 400,000.* In addition, hundreds of thousands more have passed through Mexico on their way to the United States and Canada.

---

*This study was carried out thanks to the invaluable collaboration of many individuals and institutions. Servicio, Desarrollo y Paz gave us access to its documentation. This organization and the United Nations High Commissioner for Refugees made it possible for us to administer the survey. Financing came from the Mexican Academy for Human Rights and the Hemispheric Migration Project, CIPRA of Georgetown University. I would like to highlight in particular the assistance and comments of Sergio Aguayo and Rafael González Franco; and the collaboration and support of Consuelo Díaz, Juan García, and Alfonso Jiménez de Sandi of the Refugee Studies Program at the Mexican Academy for Human Rights. Finally, special thanks go to all those Central Americans and Mexicans who generously shared their experiences with us.

With the exception of the Guatemalans located in camps in southeastern Mexico, the Central Americans are mostly undocumented and dispersed throughout Mexico. The areas of greatest concentration are along the coast of Chiapas, the cities along the U.S.-Mexico border, and Mexico City.[2]

The presence of Guatemalans on the farms of Soconusco, of Salvadorans in transit to the United States, and of Central American students, professionals, and political leaders in Mexico City is not new: nevertheless today's migration is unprecedented. The recent population movements are larger, and the demographic and social profile of the migrants becomes more diverse. Although a tradition of Central American migration existed prior to 1978, there were no signs of population movements on today's scale. As Lars Schoultz states, "this history (of Central American migration) would have to be exaggerated significantly in order to permit the conclusion that Central America can be distinguished as a region of international migration".[3]

Major efforts are underway to determine the magnitude of flows and to understand the characteristics of the recent migration to Mexico. Many studies analyze the political dimension of the population displacements. Some focus on the origin and dynamics of the migrations in order to distinguish them from traditional economic migrations. Others focus their analysis on the factors that affect government policy towards such populations, other than the legal or humanitarian considerations. The Guatemalan refugee camps have received special attention as well.[4]

In contrast, there is very little information on the dispersed refugee population, in part, because of the difficulty of obtaining data on Central Americans who try to avoid notice. Furthermore, the analytical framework of many studies (which distinguishes economic and political migrations on the basis of various pull and push factors) emphasizes the differences among migratory flows without assessing the factors in common. Many of these interpretations assume that economic migrants are compelled to migrate by poverty in their place of origin, and are attracted by the high wages and expectations of economic well-being in their destinations. Therefore, their movement is deliberate, voluntary, and often carefully planned. At the other extreme in this framework, are the refugees who are forced to leave by imminent danger to life and liberty; they are thought to have migrated with no planning, in a sort of desperate gamble.[5]

Because of these differing perceptions and in order to highlight the political nature of the Central American migration, the studies have emphasized the population's motives for leaving, which obviously are an important aspect to understanding this phenomenon. However, other aspects of displaced persons' behavior that are also important to an understanding of the current migration have been neglected. These include the selective nature of migration, those factors that influence the destination and the social networks chosen, and the integration process.

Current analytical frameworks tend to lump all Central American migrants into one seemingly homogenous group as if all shared the same motives for leaving home. However, what the Central Americans have in common, in the processe of migration away from conditions of violence and of social integration in the country of exile, is less significant than their historical, social, and educational backgrounds and their respective interpretations of their experiences at home and in exile, all of which distinguish the migrants from one another.

This paper analyzes the characteristics, behavior, living conditions, and survival strategies of Central Americans who have migrated to Mexico City since 1978. We believe this migration has its roots in the region's social conflicts, and we emphasize the diversity of the displaced population and its migratory dynamics, in comparison with other migrations.

METHODOLOGY

The present study is based on the results of a survey of 153 heads of household carried out by the Refugee Studies Program at the Mexican Academy for Human Rights from March to May, 1988.[6] (see Table 1). Interviews with 55 of the cases were held at the offices of the United Nations High Commissioner for Refugees (UNHCR), where the vast majority had documents confirming their refugee status. The other 98 interviews were conducted at the office of the Program for Assistance to Central American Refugees (PARCA), of the organization *Servicio, Desarrollo y Paz.* Of the latter, only 15 had been recognized as refugees.[7]

The survey samples are representative of: a) the Central Americans who were in touch with the offices of the UNHCR in 1988, and b) those who sought assistance from PARCA during the same period. The profile of the population interviewed at PARCA may be representative of those who establish contact with aid agencies, given that PARCA is the best-known and most extensive aid program in Mexico City. Nonetheless, the survey is not representative of the migrant population as a whole. It does not include that group of Central Americans of undeterminable size who are not in contact with UNHCR or private assistance organizations.

The surveyed population was chosen from 3,019 Central American heads of household who filled out questionnaires after approaching PARCA for assistance between 1982 and 1987. The PARCA data are an invaluable source of information; they are the only documentation that covers such a large number of cases and that gives a perspective of the population over a length of time (Table 2). However, the data obtained are not totally consistent. The responses vary due to constant changes in the questionnaire format; moreover the circumstances of the interviews may have led to falsification or exaggeration of some responses intended to improve the refugees' chances of receiving assistance.

TABLE 1

Survey Sample by Nationality, Place of Interview, Recognition as Refugees, and Migratory Status

	UNHCR		PARCA		Total Interviewed		Recognized Refugees		With Visas	
	No.	%	No.	%	No.	%	No.	%	No.	%
El Salvador	36	65.5	74	75.6	110	71.9	46	67.6	22	61.1
Guatemala	11	20.0	20	20.4	31	20.2	13	19.1	8	22.2
Honduras	6	10.9	3	3.1	9	5.9	8	11.8	6	16.7
Nicaragua	2	3.6	1	1.0	3	2.0	1	1.5	0	0.0
TOTAL	55	100.0	98	100.1	153	100.0	68	100.0	36	100.0

Source: Survey of 153 Central Americans

TABLE 2

Length of Stay in Mexico City*

	UNHCR	%	PARCA	%
More than 5 years	11	20.0	14	14.3
3 to 5 years	12	21.8	11	11.2
1 to 3 years	11	20.8	17	17.3
Less than 1 year	20	36.4	55	56.1
- 6 months to 1 year	8	14.5	10	10.2
- 3 to 6 months	4	7.3	7	7.1
- 1 to 3 months	4	7.3	23	23.5
- Less than 1 month	4	7.3	15	15.3
No answer	1	1.8	1	1.0

Source: Survey of 153 Central Americans

* The average length of stay in Mexico City at the time of the interview was calculated as 18.1 months for UNHCR contacts and 23.4 months for PARCA contacts.

Fieldwork was done in eight poor and working class communities of Mexico City where there was a notable Central American presence and where the local population opened its doors to the migrants. Church leaders, members of Christian Base Communities and the popular urban movement, families who have taken migrants into their homes, and others not involved in providing assistance were interviewed in order to gain a better understanding of the relationship between the local population and the Central Americans, the way the migrants are viewed by the community, the type of assistance provided, and the integration that has taken place. The staffs of UNHCR and the refugee assistance agencies were also interviewed.

MIGRATORY FLOWS TO MEXICO CITY

Mexico City is a magnet for Central American migration both as a final destination and a stopover on the way to the United States. There are indications of a permanent but low-level migration dating back to the 1950s. Indeed, the presence of Central American students, professionals, and political leaders has been constant. The current migration, however, is unprecedented in terms of both its size and the migrants' social origins. In a report on immigration of Central American workers to Mexico, Zazueta and Pablos state that before 1978 "with the exception of university students, there has been no substantive presence of Central Americans in the country, and practically no Central American workers."[8]

Zazueta and Pablos distinguish among three periods of Central American immigration to Mexico City. Their source is a survey of 1,205 Central American residents of the metropolitan area in 1982. Of this total, 717 were workers. The survey method overestimated the population that had resided the longest in Mexico City. The first period, prior to 1970, is almost negligible; it accounts for only 5.3 percent of their sample. The second, from 1970 to 1978, accounts for 21.8 percent of the sample. These authors conclude that this migration responded to a combination of push factors in El Salvador (economic conditions, demographic pressure, and difficult social mobility) and pull factors in Mexico City (growing demand for skilled labor). The third period, beginning in 1979, was characterized by an increase in total migration. Almost three of every four Central American workers in the sample (72.3 percent) entered the metropolitan area after 1979.[9] According to these data, with the outbreak of the Central American conflicts, annual Central American migration to Mexico City increased by over 700 percent compared to the years between 1970 and 1978 (see Table 3). The results of the 1988 survey, as illustrated in Table 4, show that the migrants tend to attribute their migration to political factors.

TABLE 3

Central American Migrant Workers by Year of Entry

Total	717	100.0
Before 1960	10	1.4
1960-1969	28	3.9
1970-1977	111	15.5
1978	45	6.3
1979	111	15.5
1980	147	20.5
1981	110	15.3
1982	151	21.1
Not Specified	4	0.6

Source: Zazueta and Pablos, Migrantes Centroamericanos en Mexico: Primer Informe Preliminar de la Encuesta de Trabajadores Centroamericanos a la República Mexicana, 1982, p. 35.

TABLE 4

Main Motives for Leaving*

	El Salvador n= 110	Guatemala n= 31	Honduras n= 9	Nicaragua n= 3
Motives %:				
- War or repression	47.0	77.4	44.0	--
- Safety threatened	69.0	67.7	55.0	100.0
- Risk to family	9.0	6.4	--	--
- Avoid recruitment	4.7	12.9	--	--
- Former prisoner	8.0	--	22.2	--
- Army deserter	--	3.2	--	--
- Guerrilla deserter	1.0	--	--	--
- Other political motives	1.0	3.2	--	--
- Economic problems	12.0	16.1	11.1	--

Source: Survey of 153 Central Americans, 1988.

*Individuals responded more than once.

This new migratory current is made up of distinct waves of migrants. The first were comprised of a relatively small group of Nicaraguans who, in 1978 and 1979, fled the escalating civil war that led to the overthrow of Anastasio Somoza. The second wave began in 1980, with a growing number of Salvadorans. Calculations of the magnitude of the migration are unreliable and inconsistent. Nevertheless, in July 1981, three months after beginning its work in Mexico, the United Nations High Commission for Refugees reported that some 70,000 Salvadorans had settled in the country. By January 1983, the UNHCR placed the figure at 120,000.[10] The estimates of non-governmental organizations were higher, ranging up to 250,000 persons, without including those who used Mexico as a stopover en route to the United States.[11]

Whatever the exact figure for Salvadorans, it was clear from the outset that large numbers had migrated to Mexico City. To attend to this population flow, a presidential decree established the Mexican Committee for Refugee Assistance (COMAR) on July 20, 1980.[12] Although formally set up to cover the needs of "foreign refugees in the National Territory," COMAR focused until mid-1982 on attending to Central Americans, especially Salvadorans, in Mexico City. In 1981, 75 percent of the refugees who received assistance from COMAR were Central Americans, of whom, 96 percent were Salvadorans. In 1983, just before COMAR suspended assistance services in Mexico City and shifted its efforts exclusively to the Guatemalan refugee camps in southeastern Mexico, Central Americans accounted for 81 percent of all refugees who received assistance from COMAR and 92 percent of these Central Americans were Salvadoran.[13] Salvadorans also accounted for a large share of the Central Americans assisted by nongovernmental organizations. For example, they accounted for 90 percent of the population assisted by the Program for Assistance to Central American Refugees (PARCA) between 1980 and 1984. Later, their number declined, as the number of Guatemalans and, to a lesser degree, Hondurans, increased. In 1987 Salvadorans accounted for 62 percent of the migration from Central America to Mexico.[14]

The Guatemalans constitute another group of migrants. There have been signs of their presence in urban areas since 1980. In 1981, parallel to the constant flow to Mexico City, another major migration was under way to the border zone of Chiapas and to Soconusco. However, their presence did not become evident in Mexico City until late 1983. From 1980 to 1982, Guatemalans accounted for less than 1.5 percent of the Central Americans assisted by COMAR in Mexico City, and 8 percent in 1983.[15] Few Guatemalans turned to PARCA before 1984, but from 1985 to 1987 Guatemalans accounted for 24 percent of the Central Americans that sought assistance from that agency.

The number of Guatemalans in Mexico City is even less certain than the range of estimates for Salvadorans. In 1984, Americas Watch and the Intergovernmental Committee for Migration (ICM) estimated that there were 7,000 Guatemalans there.[16] In 1987, the UNHCR estimated that in addition to those at the camps, there might be some 5,000 Guatemalan refugees dispersed in different parts of the country.[17] The voluntary organizations estimate that there are at least 110,000 in all of Mexico; 70,000 of whom are believed to be in Mexico City.[18]

Finally, beginning in 1983 there has been a small but growing population of Honduran and Nicaraguan migrants. From 1985 to 1987, Hondurans accounted for 7.7 percent of the total number of migrants that received assistance from PARCA. The data on Nicaraguans do not suggest a major presence in Mexico City; and the program has not had any Nicaraguan beneficiaries.[19] Nonetheless, the data on persons requesting recognition as refugees at the UNHCR offices indicates growing numbers of Nicaraguan migrants. In 1987 the number of Nicaraguans requesting such status was up twofold from 1986, and surpassed the number of Guatemalans.[20]

Tables 5 and 6 show the Central American population by nationality that has requested assistance from PARCA and UNHCR. The PARCA figures are similar to those from the UNHCR office.

An unpublished estimate on the breakdown of population by nationality is that of Johanne Gauthier for 1984, based on a survey of 110 individuals carried out by assistance agencies. According to these data, Salvadorans account for 78 percent of the population, and Guatemalans 20 percent. The investigator's estimate for Guatemalans is larger than the portion that sought assistance from PARCA that year (9.3 percent). However, the disparity may reflect the fact that until 1984 this program primarily served Salvadorans.[21]

TABLE 5

Population that Requested Assistance from PARCA, by Nationality

	Total	El Salvador	Guatemala	Honduras	Nicaragua
	(%)	(%)	(%)	(%)	(%)
1982	299 (10.4)	298 (99.7)	-- ---	-- ---	1 (0.3)
1983	258 (8.9)	247 (95.7)	5 (1.9)	3 (1.2)	3 (1.2)
1984	656 (22.7)	558 (85.1)	61 (9.3)	34 (5.2)	3 (0.5)
1985	450 (15.1)	279 (62.0)	124 (27.5)	22 (4.9)	25 (5.6)
1986	735 (24.7)	463 (63.0)	177 (24.1)	62 (8.4)	33 (4.5)
1987	574 (19.3)	406 (70.7)	113 (19.7)	52 (9.1)	3 (0.5)
Total 2972		2251 (75.7)	480 (16.2)	173 (5.8)	68 (2.3)

Source: PARCA, 1982-1987 (does not include 37 cases, as the information regarding the date of registration at PARCA is not clear)

TABLE 6

Population Seeking UNHCR Recognition by Nationality

	Total	El Salvador	Guatemala	Honduras	Nicaragua
		(%)	(%)	(%)	(%)
1985	943	620 (65.7)	185 (19.6)	29 (3.1)	109 (11.6)
1986	821	508 (61.9)	158 (19.2)	44 (5.4)	111 (13.5)
1987	920	515 (56.0)	101 (11.0)	52 (5.7)	252 (27.4)

Source: UNHCR. Report of Protection Activities 1985, 1986, 1987 (does not include previous years, as the information was not broken down by nationality).

CHARACTERISTICS OF THE MIGRANT POPULATION

In studying the demographic profile and the social origins of the migrant population we find that recent Central American migration to Mexico City represents a qualitative as well as quantitative transformation. The Central Americans who traditionally migrated to Mexico City were young men of urban origin, with average years of schooling that are high for the region (over 12 years).[22] Beginning in 1978, as the Central American conflicts worsened, the number of migrants increased and the overall proportion of single young men began to decline as more women and dependents, children and elderly migrated. Education levels dropped and, although most migrants still come from urban centers, their occupational background has shifted from the professions and universities to the service sector.

For example, according to Table 7, the average educational level of Central American migrants from countries without major conflicts (Belize, Costa Rica, Honduras, and Panama), is quite high (12.7), much greater than the average for the country of origin or for Mexico City; these migrants, who were interviewed in 1982, are representative of traditional labor migration. In contrast, educational levels are lower (11.3 years) among the migrants from more conflictive countries (El Salvador, Guatemala, and Nicaragua), where the push factors are more acute. Among the former, there is no illiteracy, and those with a college education account for 47.1 percent of the total. In the conflictive countries the college-educated group falls to 31.2 percent, and there are some illiterates (3.2 percent).

Other sources suggest that the migrants' educational levels went down in later years. Table 7 also shows that the average education of Salvadoran and Guatemalan heads of household (who received assistance from September to December 1983) was slightly above eighth grade level. The college educated accounted for 13 percent of the total, illiterates for 3 percent.[23]

TABLE 7

Educational Levels

	Migration* up to 1982 Levels of Conflict		1983** Guatemala and El Salvador	1988***
	Low(a)	High(b)		
Number of Cases	153	564	155	149
None	-	3.2	3.2	8.7
Primary	8.5	13.5	45.8	37.5
Secondary	18.3	23.4	16.7	23.4
Post-secondary	19.0	23.4	26.4	24.8
University	47.1	31.2	7.7	6.0

Source: *   Zazueta and Pablos, op. cit., p. 29
         ** COMAR, Informe de Actividades, September-December, 1983
         *** Survey of 153 Central Americans

(a) Low Conflict Countries include Belize, Costa Rica, Honduras and Panama.

(b) High Conflict Countries include Guatemala, El Salvador, and Nicaragua.

Our survey indicates that the average educational level of the population seeking assistance in 1988 was still eighth grade. Nonetheless, the number of those with a college education declined with respect to previous figures, while the illiteracy rate increased.

In short, in the last ten years the migration of Central Americans has diversified and has come to include broad sectors of the population. Nonetheless, it is still highly selective: only a portion of the hundreds of thousands of persons displaced by the violence choose Mexico City as their destination. And this portion tends to be better educated, from urban areas, and includes a greater number of working age (or draft age) males.

Several conditions in Mexico City favor migration: the country's political stability, proximity and relatively open borders;[24] its accessible routes and affordable travel;[25] the tradition of migration among Central American students and politicians; and with the increase in the number of migrants, the reception networks for relatives and fellow citizens have also grown; the city offers many educational opportunities and greater employment opportunities than other cities in Mexico; and Mexico exerts considerable cultural influence in Central America.[26] Nevertheless, not everyone has the same opportunity to travel. In each migration that involves diverse circumstances and motives, there are common factors that condition mobility (see Table 8). Some of the factors analyzed in this section include: the age and number of children or dependents; the place of origin; educational background; and the economic sector of origin.

Demographic Profile

The demographic profile of migrants is a clear indicator of the change in the nature of the current Central American migration. The results of our survey conducted at the offices of UNHCR and PARCA -- 153 cases, 362 individuals -- indicate a very broad demographic displacement. We found a significant number of women and dependents, who are individuals that do not normally take part in economic migration. Nonetheless, the mobility of migrants is conditioned in a similar way as other migrations, and therefore, the migrants remain a highly selective group.

TABLE 8

Main Reasons for Choosing Mexico City as a Destination

	El Salvador n= 110	Guatemala n= 31	Honduras n= 9	Nicaragua n=3
Reasons (in percentage):				
- To join relatives	16.8	3.2	--	--
- Presence of fellow citizens	17.8	9.6	11.1	--
- Ease of obtaining employment	32.2	36.6	11.1	--
Opportunity to study	6.9	9.6	--	--
To go unnoticed	3.9	6.4	11.1	--
Existence of services	3.9	3.2	--	75.0
Other	19.0	25.8	33.3	25.0
N.A.	--	5.4	33.3	--

Source: Survey of 153 Central Americans, 1988

Some 59.4 percent of the population surveyed were men and 40.6 percent women (see Table 9). In breaking down the data by age one observes that: a) 29 percent are 15 years of age or under, and b) 60 percent are part of the economically active age range of 16 to 45 years.

Young people who migrated alone account for 52.9 percent of the cases, (85 percent are males, and 15 percent females), which explains in part the high percentage of people between the ages of 15 to 30. The remaining 47 percent of the heads of household migrated in families with an average size of 4 members. Of these: a) 49 percent are couples with or without children, and at times with another immediate relative, usually a grandparent; b) 28 percent are single-parent families (93 percent of these cases are single mothers with children); and c) the remaining 21 percent are new family units, made up of what remains of extended families profoundly affected by the war. These extended families are comprised of siblings, in-laws, or, for example, a head of household, his or her nephews, and his or her grandmother.

This demographic profile reveals clear differences between the surveyed group and other migrations of undocumented, and generally economically motivated, individuals. First, the demographic profile in Table 9 presents a different male-female ratio. For the population we studied, the ratio of men to women is 146. Almost 3 men for every two women, which is considerably smaller than the usual male-female ratio among other undocumented migrations, in which men generally predominate in economic migrations of undocumented persons. For example, in the case of undocumented Mexican migrants to the United States in 1977 and 1978, the male-female ratio was estimated at 521. In contrast, the profile of the population under study here is similar to that of the legal migrations of Mexicans and Central Americans to the United States, whose ratios are 109 and 167, respectively, for 1977.[27]

In addition, the existing data, indicates that over the years the number of females has increased among Central American migrants. Zazueta and Pablos (1982) put the male-female ratio for all Central American migrants at 206, explaining that this ratio was greater than the ration for exclusively legal migration (estimated at 167). Zazueta and Pablos indicated that as more illegal Central Americans migrated to Mexico, more men would migrate in relation to women.[28] Nonetheless, despite the steady increase in the number of undocumented

TABLE 9

Age Distribution of Surveyed Household Population

Age	Males	Females	Total	(%)	Male-Female ratio*
0 - 10	40	27	67	(.19)	148
11 - 15	19	18	37	(.10)	105
16 - 20	32	15	47	(.13)	213
21 - 25	40	25	65	(.18)	160
26 - 30	30	18	48	(.13)	166
31 - 35	20	6	26	(.07)	333
36 - 40	8	12	20	(.06)	66
41 - 45	7	4	11	(.03)	175
46 - 50	7	7	14	(.04)	100
51 - 60	7	10	17	(.05)	70
Over 61	5	5	10	(.03)	100
Total	215	147	362		146
Percent	59.4	40.6	100.0		

Source: Survey of 153 Central Americans

*Number of males for every 100 females

migrants, our survey reveals the disproportion between the sexes to be less pronounced than have been predicted.

The percentage of Central Americans who migrate alone, though high, is less than in the case of undocumented Mexican migrants to the United States. The average age of Central Americans is higher (27.8 years), and there is also a higher percentage of dependents among the former; 28.7 percent are children and 11.3 percent are retired adults.[29]

In light of this data, one may conclude that the massive presence of Central Americans in Mexico City is a new phenomenon, linked to the conflicts in the region, and that it is not simply an increase in the traditional pattern economic migration. The demographic profile of these migrants has changed. The average age for adult migrants is higher, and there are more women and children. These are characteristics more typically associated with legal migration or migration resulting from natural disasters or widespread violence.

However, there is still a major trend toward selectivity in the migration to Mexico City. Data on internally displaced Salvadorans and Salvadoran refugees in Costa Rica and Nicaragua prepared by the "Simeón Cañas" Central American University (UCA) of El Salvador in 1984 helps illustrate this tendency.[30] First, among Salvadorans in Mexico City there is a predominance of migrants without family and of small nuclear families of migrants, with only an average of 2.2 family members. In contrast, the internally displaced in El Salvador live in extended family units (8.6 family members on average) with a large number of children. The average number of family members among the Salvadoran refugees in Costa Rica and Nicaragua is 5.9.

Moreover, the UCA study found that the further the destination, the fewer number of children, and the greater the number of economically active persons who took part. Children under 12, and the economically active population ages 19 to 65, account respectively for 37 and 44 percent of internally-displaced Salvadorans; 30 and 50 percent respectively among Salvadoran refugees in Nicaragua and Costa Rica; and 21 and 60 percent respectively in Mexico City.

Place of Origin

The dual tendency of Central American migration to Mexico City, of incorporating new groups while conserving its selective nature, becomes clear in the analysis of the migrants' place of origin. As in the past, most of the Central American migrants (59 percent) are from urban centers with populations over 15,000. The rest, almost unknown to Mexico City until the late 1970s, are from medium-size rural population centers, or semi-urban areas, with a population of 5,000 to 15,000 (34 percent), and from population centers with less than 5,000 inhabitants.

Unlike Central American refugees, living in camps in Mexico and Honduras, who represent a rather small number of towns and villages in border areas, migrants to Mexico City are from a wide variety of places in their own countries.[31] The lack of a large group or community makes life difficult and insecure; there are few people the emigrants feel they can trust. While they do assist one another, they generally do not participate in social activities outside their immediate group of friends and family. Furthermore, the fact that the Central Americans in Mexico City are from many different places complicates the prospects for repatriation. (See section on prospects for return below.)

The Central Americans interviewed include Salvadorans from all 14 departments, with a predominance from San Salvador (29 percent), La Libertad (17 percent), Santa Ana (12 percent), Usulután (10 percent), Sonsonate (7 percent), and San Vicente (6 percent). Almost half of the Guatemalan migrants are from the department of Guatemala in the central part of the country (48 percent); others came from San Marcos (13 percent), Escuintla in the south (10 percent), Jutiapa in the east (6 percent), and El Petén in the north (3 percent).

There are relatively few Hondurans and Nicaraguans. The Hondurans in the survey represent seven departments, mainly Yoro and Cortez. However, there are few migrants from the capital, Tegucigalpa although all of the Nicaraguans are from Managua.

Educational Background

The migrants to Mexico City generally have a high educational level. Seventy-six percent have had some formal schooling, only 24 percent have not. However, four-fifths of this latter group are children under 10 years of age; only 5 percent of the migrants surveyed are adults with no education. Thirty-eight percent have completed some level of primary education, and 17 percent some level of secondary education.

Only a small percentage of Guatemalans and Salvadorans in their own countries have such educational levels, which are higher than those of the displaced and refugee population as a whole. In Guatemala, for example, 52 percent of the population over 10 years of age is illiterate;[32] in El Salvador 50 percent of the population over 7 years of age is illiterate.[33] According to the UCA report, half of the internally displaced persons in El Salvador are illiterate, but in Mexico City only 22 percent of the Salvadoran migrants are. Among the internally displaced only 5 percent have been to junior high school, 1 percent to high school; whereas among Salvadorans living in Mexico City these figures are 20 percent and 16 percent, respectively.

Economic Background

As observed in Table 10, the migrants worked in the service sector (mechanics, drivers, office workers), were students, and, in third place worked in agriculture before migrating.

Approximately 52 percent of the Salvadorans and 58 percent of the Guatemalans worked in the service sector. However, 26 percent of the Guatemalans and 20 percent of the Salvadorans worked in agriculture. The families of other migrants worked in construction, small businesses, and manufacturing.

This trend indicates a marked selectivity of the migrant population. Whereas in Guatemala 57 percent of the total population worked in agriculture and 12.5 percent in services as of 1976 the proportions were reversed for migrants. The same occurred in El Salvador, where almost 60 percent of the population worked in agriculture in 1974.[34]

Table 10

Occupation in Place of Origin

	Interviewee		Other Family Members	
	No.	%	No.	%
Agriculture	21	13.8	28	7.7
Manufacturing	3	2.0	3	.8
Small Commerce	7	4.6	9	2.5
Construction	15	9.9	19	5.2
Services	76	50.0	128	35.4
Students	29	18.9	93	25.7
Other	1	.7	1	.3
None*	--	--	81	22.4
Total	152	--	362	100.0

Source: Survey of 153 Central Americans

* Includes the population that was not economically active, women who do not work outside the home and elderly persons.

In comparing this trend with the results of the UCA study we see that the percentage of displaced persons of peasant origin declines as distance from the place of origin increases. Whereas in El Salvador 81 percent of displaced persons are from the agricultural sector, in Nicaragua and Costa Rica the percentage is only 34 percent, and only 19 percent in the results of the Mexico City survey. A recent study on Salvadoran migration to the United States indicates that only 12 percent of the Salvadoran migrants to the U.S. are from the agricultural sector.[35] (See Table 11 below).

TABLE 11

Rural Displaced Salvadorans by Current Location, Subsistence on Land and Migration

Location	Rural Origin %	Subsistence on Land %	Migrant Labor Households %
El Salvador*	80.8	40.2	59.6
Costa Rica and Nicaragua*	34.2	38.1	30.8
Mexico City**	19.1	14.2	23.8

Source: * UCA, 1985, p. 199

**Survey of 153 Central Americans, 1988

Note: *Columns 2 and 3 list percentages from rural displaced population and not from total displaced population.*

The UCA data also suggest that destination is closely related to available resources. Forty percent of the internally displaced did not have enough land to live on for more than six months out of the year, but only 14 percent of the refugees in Mexico City had so little land. Moreover, the internally displaced were under more pressure to migrate within their own countries to earn income. Thus, there are fewer peasants among the migrants in Mexico City than in other destinations. Those peasants who do migrate Mexico City are relatively better off than the internally displaced in El Salvador and or the Salvadoran refugees in Costa Rica and Nicaragua; the former had more or better land, and before the war they migrated less frequently to complement their incomes.

Migration in Stages

Previous data on migrants' place of origin, social background, and schooling suggests that those who migrate to Mexico City constitute a select group of the thousands of people affected by the conflicts. The final element in support of the selective migration hypothesis derives from the profile of migration "in stages."

Most of the Central Americans (i.e., all of the Hondurans, 85 percent of the Salvadorans, 71 percent of the Guatemalans, and 70 percent of the Nicaraguans) arrived in Mexico City directly from their places of origin. The rest made the trip over a period of several months. Mexico City marked the end of a long and difficult journey for them. This group migrated "in stages" because it lacked the information, money, and contacts to go directly.

Chiapas is for such migrants a very frequent stop-over. There they may spend two to five months. Others pass through different Mexican states, including Campeche, Tabasco, Puebla, Hidalgo, Quintana Roo, and Veracrúz.

The "stopover migrants" are more vulnerable than the rest of the Central Americans refugees interviewed. Their educational levels are lower -- 6.3 years of study for Salvadorans, and 5.3 for Guatemalans (compared to 8.7 and 7.8 years respectively for the sample as a whole), and 40 percent of the "stopover migrants" are illiterate.

Moreover, a higher percentage of the "stopover migrants" are from the countryside: 27 percent of the Salvadorans and 67 percent of the Guatemalans. Service workers, who account for more than half of the migrants in the sample, are a minority among these migrants (see Table 12 below).

TABLE 12

Migrant Employment by Sector
Overall and Among "Stopover Migrants"
(in percentage)

	El Salvador		Guatemala	
	General	"Stopovers"	General	"Stopovers"
	N = 110	N = 11	N = 31	N = 91
Agriculture	19	27	26	67
Manufacturing	5	18	3	--
Small Commerce	7	9	3	--
Construction	9	18	6	11
Services	52	9	58	22
No Response	8	19	4	--

Source: Survey of 153 Central Americans, 1988

SURVIVAL STRATEGIES

The surveyed Central Americans have migrated to one of the largest cities in the world with 18 million inhabitants. Though most are from urban areas, they still experience a radical change upon arrival to Mexico City. Most do not have migration papers, so they try to remain anonymous and mix in with the rest of the local population, or with Mexicans from southeastern Mexico who arrive in Mexico City seeking work. Thus, as with all migrants, the new situations they face in Mexico City -- for example, differences in vocabulary and turns of phrase they are not familiar with, difficulty in figuring out how to use the currency, lack of information, and differences in customs -- constitute a heavy burden that generate anguish and distrust. Finding housing, work, medical care and school for their children are almost impossible tasks. In this situation it is difficult to overcome the experience of fear and loss -- having abandoned family, friends, the dead, and their land. In order to survive, the Central Americans must live in silence and disguise their true identity.

Although they account for a large percentage of all the displaced Central Americans, the Central Americans in Mexico City account for only a small fraction of the thousands of people who move to Mexico City each year to continue their studies or look for work. In 1980, for example, some 200,000 Mexicans migrated to the city from different parts of the country.[36]

Students of this Mexican migration to the capital agree that the decisive factor in migration and integration in the city is the presence there of a relative. Relatives provide housing and food to new arrivals, and serve as contacts for getting a first job and independent housing.[37]

In a certain sense, the Central Americans join this flow of Mexican migrants, and they survive. Nonetheless, the results of the survey showed that only 22 percent of the Salvadorans had relatives in

Mexico City. So, where do the rest go when they arrive, and how are they integrated?

First Contacts

According to the survey data, only 26 percent of the Guatemalans and 49 percent of the Salvadorans had references for fellow countrymen or Mexicans in Mexico City who would be willing to help them on their arrival. However, before arriving, most of the Central Americans had either made a contact or obtained information about Mexicans or Central Americans to whom they could turn. Seventy percent of the Salvadorans have contact with other Salvadorans; 26 percent with Mexicans. Some 40 percent of the Guatemalans, on the other hand, turn to fellow countrymen, and a similar percentage to Mexicans.

These data suggest that Salvadorans have developed more extensive social networks than Guatemalans. According to the interviews, they have twice as many contacts as Guatemalans in Mexico City; in half of the cases these contacts are close relatives. Guatemalans, on the other hand, have few contacts, whether with other Guatemalans or Mexicans. Not one of them has said that he or she has other relatives who had migrated earlier. Thus, when they arrived in Mexico City they are more dependent on assistance from Mexicans.

There are several reasons why Salvadorans have such strong networks and other nationality groups do not. Even though there were very few Central Americans in Mexico City (and these consisted of almost exclusively of students and professionals) before 1978 the metropolitan area has always been a stopover point for Salvadoran migrants bound for the United States. Moreover, there are more Salvadorans, increasingly so since 1980, whereas the Guatemalan presence has only been notable since 1983 and 1984. There are few, if any, support networks for the small number of Nicaraguans and Hondurans who have arrived more recently; but they use the same networks as the other Central Americans, especially the Salvadorans. These relations among Central Americans of different nationalities generally occur at the nongovernmental organizations where assistance is provided, and where Central Americans meet, talk, and share their experiences and their resources--basically social contacts and information.

For the majority of Central Americans, the first contact is fundamental. Sixty-two percent of the Central Americans solve their housing needs this way, whether the contacted family receives the migrants in its home at no cost (as in 55 percent of our sample) or helps them obtain housing (12.4 percent of our sample). In this regard, the participation of the local population is extremely important. Fifty percent of those interviewed who had been in Mexico City for less than a month lived with Mexicans, while only 20 percent lived with Central Americans. Of those who had been in the city for more than 6 months, 13 percent lived with Mexicans and 17 percent with Central Americans.

For 25 percent of those interviewed the first contact led to valuable information; for 34 percent, some type of assistance, mainly economic; and for 13 percent, help in finding a job.

The results of the PARCA questionnaires (Table 13) confirm the importance of first contacts in finding housing. Fifty seven percent of the population that seeks assistance during the first month in the city lives at no cost with Mexican and Central American families. Even after a year, one of every five Central Americans depends on the hospitality of others for housing.

In the open-ended interviews Central Americans stated that their first social contacts were very important for survival in the first months after arrival. The following testimony of a Guatemalan woman who migrated in 1984, is a typical example:

> Arrival in Mexico City was a sad experience
> for me. I didn't know the streets, the city, or
> people I could trust. I was afraid of being in
> another country because of the vocabulary,
> handling money ... how you buy tortillas-- we
> didn't know anything. We spent a week lost
> here in Mexico City. We couldn't find any
> contacts....Thanks to a Central American man
> I got to Xochimilco, where a Mexican woman
> received me. Other Mexicans gave me some
> old cots, without mattresses, and some plastic
> cups. People gave me clothes. The owner of

TABLE 13

Type of Housing by Length of Stay in Mexico City

Total n= 2,909	Less than 1 month n= 1,508	1-3 months n= 558	3-6 months n= 331	6-12 months n= 214	More than 12 months n= 298
	(%)	(%)	(%)	(%)	(%)
Rent	18.2	36.3	49.6	57.4	66.4
Guest in home	57.1	45.8	35.3	29.4	22.1
Work	3.3	3.9	4.8	3.2	1.6
Live in the street	7.3	2.1	1.2	.9	.3
Hostel/Dormitory	8.2	8.0	5.5	2.6	2.9
No response	5.9	3.9	3.6	6.5	6.7

Source: PARCA. 1982-1987 (does not include 100 cases because the information on housing is not clear).

the house and his wife called us when it was
time to eat....With time I managed ways to support my daughters. I sold tamales in the
street, and tacos. I didn't know what tacos
were, but a woman taught me and explained
them to me.

The Role of Mexican Communities

Many of the Mexicans who take Central Americans into their
homes live in poor, working class communities organized around a
Protestant or Catholic church. Refugee assistance is new in some
neighborhoods. In others it dates back to 1973, with the arrival of
Chileans. But it was not until 1979, in connection with the revolution-
ary process in Nicaragua and the death later of Monsignor Oscar Ar-
nulfo Romero, that most of the parishes we visited began to take
people in. These communities had study groups or solidarity groups
on the Central American conflict and decided to receive immigrants
as an expression of solidarity.

From 1979 to 1983, acceptance of the first migrants in the
communities was promoted by a sense of euphoria among those following and supporting the Central American struggle. The media
gave extensive coverage to Nicaragua's political-military problems,
and the foreign policy of the national leadership broke with Mexico's
tradition of isolation from and neutrality toward the problems in
Central America.[38] There were solidarity weeks, demonstrations, and
other public activities in support of Central America, but these
tapered off after 1984.[39]

The reception process was similar in the eight communities
where we conducted interviews. The community's first contact with
Central Americans occurred when a family or small group of migrants
sought asylum in the church. Generally, the migrants did this on the
recommendation of a pastoral worker or a representative of a nongovernmental organization in Central America who had contacts with
the parish in Mexico. These first migrants, usually catechists or community leaders, were received in the parish or the home of a family involved in pastoral work. Many were university students, mid-level
professionals, trade unionists or members of student or peasant organizations or cooperatives. Some migrated to the United States or

were accepted by resettlement programs, usually in Canada.[40] They became integrated into the community with relative ease through their participation in church activities. Their contacts with other solidarity groups, in the place of origin and in Mexico, made them good liaisons for other migrants.

The presence of these first Central Americans drew others. Word of finding refuge spreads quickly among the networks of Central Americans, churches, and aid agencies. The parish community would organize room and board for some of those who sought assistance from the parish, whether in the church or through families. The parish would also provide clothes and economic assistance, and locate independent housing and work for the new arrivals. In general, the work has consisted of temporary jobs such as stone masons, bakery and shop helpers, machine operators, street vendors, and household help.

As the number of Central Americans grew-- in 1984 and 1985 some communities received as many as 15 or 20 families--their presence came to be seen as troublesome in all the communities visited. In these years Central Americans began arriving in greater numbers, without recommendations or any orientation whatsoever. Most did not participate in the conflicts, but did suffer from the violence and its economic consequences.[41] Few succeeded in winning recognition as refugees, obtaining legal status, or participating in resettlement programs. In addition, the exacerbation of the economic crisis in Mexico made it difficult for them to get by without assistance from Mexicans. The local population, itself suffering from the increase of unemployment and the raising and cost of living, had often questioned the wisdom of providing assistance. Indeed, two years after the Central Americans presence mushroomed, assistance programs in seven of the eight communities visited were reduced and the criteria for choosing beneficiaries were tightened.

Moreover, the context that justified the reception programs has gradually changed. The programs began in the wake of the Sandinista revolution, as an expression of support for the struggle in Central America and under the assumption that the migration would be short-term. Since late 1982, the idea of a victorious revolution in El Salvador and Guatemala has become doubtful. Central America attracts less attention from the general population sectors, and media interest has declined.

At present, the relationship between the communities and the Central Americans is not very good. To most of the Mexicans interviewed the assistance provided by their parish is inexplicable. The Mexicans who opposed the Central American presence in their communities from the outset feel freer to express their opposition. There are indications that false accusations against the migrants have been made to the police. Indeed, families who put up Central Americans in their homes and spoke positively of the experience now blame them for many problems.

In some cases, the presence of large numbers of Central Americans set off latent conflicts in the communities. For example, in one of the communities visited, despite the presence of relatively few Central Americans, conflicts occurred over the control of church activities between the recently formed Christian Base Communities and the group that had traditionally cared for the Church. The Base Community, supported by the priest, had promoted the formation of Bible study groups and sought to build networks for participation and solidarity within the community; one of these was the project to organize assistance for Central Americans. In practice, these activities had isolated from the Church those who traditionally took charge of the popular devotions. Everyday problems of coexistence and integration arose as more and more Central Americans came to the community, and these problems were used by the traditional groups to cast doubt on the overall work of the Christian Base community before the higher Church authorities. In the end, these groups succeeded in removing from the church the priest who had unconditionally supported the base community and inspired the reception of the Central Americans. Today the Central American assistance program is very small and does not enjoy the unequivocal support of the church.

In recent years Central Americans have not generally been considered worthy of welcome. In contrast to the idealized image of the first Central Americans-- who were active in the Church and politically aware *(concientizados)*-- the new migrants are accused of not participating in community activities, taking advantage of the assistance, drinking, not working, and stealing. Statements along the following lines are quite common:

> The first ones were morally and spiritually upright, although some were from other churches. Now they are morally impoverished....

The first ones had a great sense of community, leaving the doors of their Mexican hosts open to receive other people, especially from El Salvador. Nonetheless, things change. Those who come now commit crimes (although the interviewee did not specify which ones). They don't work, they get drunk in front of everyone else -- they disdain our country. It is difficult to bring yourself to open your door to them.

This image, which makes the migrants' lives all the more difficult, coincides with that conveyed by the media. The largest circulation newspapers in Mexico City -- *La Prensa* and *Ovaciones,* some radio stations, and recently commercial television, refer to the Central American migration as a public safety and employment problem, associating the Central Americans with common crime, drug trafficking, and prostitution.[42] Here is a representative item from the afternoon edition of *Ovaciones*:

At present it is estimated that six thousand foreigners enter our territory every 15 days. Of these, only 1,800 are repatriated monthly. The rest make it to the United States, settle in the country displacing Mexican labor, or take part in crime, prostitution, and drugs.[43]

Other reports state that their objective is to destabilize the country. For example, the daily paper *La Prensa* has stated that:

Many of them (illegal Central and South Americans) are undesirable and pernicious elements, who engage in agitation and indoctrination. Some are subversives who incite our citizens to conflict in order to cause social imbalances and cause protests that these "visitors" deem appropriate....It is said that they have been sponsored in their subversive work by opposition political organizations which, lacking national support or sympathy, seem to bolster themselves with those who ar-

rive; perhaps that is why they help them to
make a mockery of our migration laws, shelter-
ing and protecting them.[44]

The Role of Nongovernmental Organizations (NGOs)

Along with the solidarity of some Mexicans, whether spon-
taneous or organized in church groups, nongovernmental organizations and new programs in established NGOs have sprung up in
Mexico City since 1980. These provide shelter, emergency relief, legal
counsel, and job opportunities for Central American migrants. Although their coverage has been limited, they have played an important
role in providing referral services and assistance to the migrants and
in acting as intermediaries with the authorities.

The Central Americans turn to the assistance agencies with a
wide variety of needs that according to the survey results, can be
grouped into four categories: First is emergency material aid--
money, food, and clothes-- which is provided by the agencies that have
the broad coverage, PARCA and *Casa de los Amigos*. PARCA,
provides a one-time monetary allowance for four consecutive weeks as
well as clothes and in some cases, money to pay rent. Second, there
are numerous demands for legal assistance that are attended to by the
vast majority of the agencies. Of the agencies mentioned by the
Central Americans in the survey, only the Office of Legal Protection
(Socorro Jurídico) provides this assistance to Salvadorans, and the
Center for Studies and Social Promotion to persons being resettled in
Canada. There are other organizations, such as the Mexican League
for Human Rights, and Development and Human Promotion, which
were not mentioned by the Central Americans, that are also engaged
in legal defense work. A third need is health care. PARCA and some
parish clinics provide primary medical care.

Finally, there are also longer-term demands for housing,
employment, and productive projects. Housing and employment
demands are occasionally met when there is an announcement of job
opportunities for Central Americans or when information is received
about a Mexican community willing to receive migrants. Some agencies are carrying out productive projects, including Vluchkteling,
PARCA, and the Center for Studies and Social Promotion; but these
projects involve a limited number of migrants. In general, these

demands are met indirectly, i.e., the agencies serve as meeting places for the exchange of information among a highly dispersed population.

From 1980 to 1984 the nongovernmental agencies also operated hostels to facilitate initial contacts for the migrants. According to people who have worked with the nongovernmental organizations and solidarity groups, these hostels were essential for many migrants. Although less numerous than in later years, most were directly linked to popular organizations or church groups. Often, for example, parish groups in El Salvador provided references and recommended people to agencies in Mexico City.

In 1985, citing various reasons, the nongovernmental organizations began to close most of the hostels. PARCA argued that it faced difficulties running its hostel, and that it no longer fulfilled its role as a stopover, as many migrants ended up staying for prolonged periods. Other organizations closed hostels because of the decline in demand for lodging from newly arrived migrants. Ever fewer Central Americans were using the agencies' reception channels, although they did continue to seek other assistance. This suggests that the reception networks for Central Americans have become stronger, whether they function through communities in the city, individual Mexicans, or other Central Americans; and also, that the number of Central Americans sent directly from their country of origin to solidarity groups in Mexico has declined. In addition, even those "recommended" began to use other contacts for their initial reception.

The loss of contact of nongovernmental organizations with the arriving migrants has resulted in a shift in the work of these organizations. Migrants now approach them to seek assistance when unemployed or to supplement their incomes. In addition, the relationship between the organizations and the Central Americans has become short-term. The only on-going link is through health services and, for a minority, through the productive projects.

Table 14 summarizes the results of the survey with regard to first contacts and contacts used by the migrants to decide in which community to live and work. Table 15, on survival mechanisms during periods of unemployment, illustrates the reduced role of the agencies in the initial reception, and their importance as a mechanism for supplementing incomes.

TABLE 14

ontacts Used by Arriving Migrants to Obtain Employment and Decide Where to Settle

of Contact	First Contact		Obtain Employment		Obtain Housing	
	Salv.	Guat.	Salv.	Guat.	Salv.	Guat.
nitiative	--	--	28.2	29.0	33.6	32.3
w Citizen	53.6	29.3	10.9	3.2	45.5	12.9
Central icans	10.0	9.6	1.8	--	2.7	9.7
ans	26.3	35.4	10.9	19.4	13.5	35.5
h	--	--	.9	--	--	3.2
tance Agency	--	--	2.7	3.2	2.7	--
	--	--	--	3.2	--	--
	6.4	7.1	43.6	41.9	--	--
	3.7	18.6	--	--	2.0	6.4

: Survey of 153 Central American, 1988

TABLE 15

Survival Strategies in Periods of Unemployment*

	Salvadorans	Guatemalans
Savings	9.1	12.9
Other members' work	19.1	3.2
Aid from Central Americans	13.6	12.9
Loans from neighbors	5.5	3.2
Aids from church	5.5	6.5
Aid from agencies	38.2	25.8
Other types of aid	17.3	22.6
No Response	10.9	22.6

Source: Survey of 153 Central Americans, 1988

*Some individuals responded more than once.

LEGAL STATUS

Legal status is an element that influences the social relations of Central Americans and their ability to integrate into Mexican society. Mexico is not party to the 1951 Convention on the Status of Refugees, nor to the additional Protocol of 1967; and Mexican legislation does not allow for refugee status.[45] Nevertheless, Mexico has signed the San José Pact and other international treaties that prohibit the extradition of persons in danger of persecution in their place of origin,[46] and the goverment allowed the establishment of an office of the United Nations High Commissioner on Refugees in Mexico City in March 1981, and later, the establishment of offices in the areas of the camps.

This combination of policies led to a complex legal situation for the Central Americans and posed a fundamental contradiction. On the one hand, since 1981 the UNHCR office in Mexico City has extended a certificate recognizing their status as refugees to Central Americans who so request and, after an individual interview and case-by-case evaluation, who it believes have a well-founded fear of persecution for reasons of race, religion, nationality, or adhering to a particular social group or political belief. This certificate establishes that:

> ...(said person) of (said nationality) is a
> refugee under the mandate of the United Na-
> tions High Commissioner for Refugees, in ac-
> cordance with the terms of the Statute of the
> Office of the UNHCR, Annex to Resolution
> 428 (V) of the United Nations General As-
> sembly of 14 December 1950.[47] This certifi-
> cate, which is valid for 6 months from the date
> of issue, is issued as proof of holder's status as
> a refugee.

However, this document has no legal effect and does not lead, under the General Law on Population, to a granting of Mexican immigration status. Refugees are placed in the same category as any other foreigner, enjoying no special privileges. By virtue of their social background and precarious economic situation, the vast majority cannot comply with the requirements established by law for obtaining official immigration status. To obtain such status, one must present proof of a relatively high income from sources other than work abroad (two to three times the minimum wage), or one must have been asked to work in an area of Mexican national interest which would not displace Mexican labor. Legalization is practically impossible for the vast majority of Central Americans, who have no economic resources of their own and limited opportunities for scholarships, and who are looking for work in the same activities as thousands of unemployed Mexicans. Furthermore, a large group of Central Americans cannot even request this status because they are undocumented; by law one must have a valid visa in order to apply for another one.

Nevertheless, the Mexican government was interested in winning international recognition for its tradition of asylum, and on several occasions officials of the Ministries of Interior and Foreign Relations reiterated their respect for the principle of *nonrefoulement*.* In theory this should protect the refugees recognized by the UNHCR and those who, at the time of arrest, are seeking such recognition, even if they are not documented. While there is no evidence of Central Americans recognized as refugees by the UNHCR being returned, no legal mechanisms have been established to guarantee unrestricted compliance with this principle. Thus, the Central Americans who have not gone to the UNHCR, and who generally are not aware of their rights, are not informed of their rights if they are detained. Moreover, access to prisons and detention centers by representatives of the UNHCR and nongovernmental organizations is the decision of the particular official in charge.

Any problem which might have arisen from the contradiction between the lack of a legal framework for protection and formal respect for the principle of *nonrefoulement* have been partially resolved through the maintenance of an ambiguous policy. From 1979

---

*The principle of not returning to their place of origin people whose life or liberty might be endangered.

to May 1981, when the first Guatemalans arrived across the southern
border and were then deported, the authorities supported the
Nicaraguan and Salvadoran presence in Mexico City; and did not appear to opposed offering them protection. As we have seen, institutions such as COMAR were established for the expressed aim of
serving this population. The March 1981 Agreement of cooperation
under which the Mexican authorities invited the United Nations High
Commissioner on Refugees to assist the refugee population, establishes that:

> bearing in mind the large number of asylees
> and refugees presently in Mexico, especially
> the new groups coming from Central
> America, the Mexican Committee for
> Refugee Assistance and the Office of the
> United Nations High Commissioner for
> Refugees agree to cooperate closely in the for-
> mulation and financing of programs to assist
> asylees and refugees, who fall within the
> policy on this matter as defined by the
> Mexican authorities regarding the number of
> refugees, their reception, placement, occupa-
> tion, and stay, as well as within the framework
> of fundamental internationally recognized
> laws in this area.[48]

Two months after the UNHCR office was established in
Mexico City, the massive arrival of the first Guatemalans to the
southern border caused serious disagreements between the Ministry
of Foreign Relations, which was committed to an active foreign policy
in Central America, and the Ministry of Interior, which through the
Office of Migratory Affairs had often noted the economic nature of
the Central American migration. Until mid-1982, many Guatemalans
who attempted to reach the camps inside the Mexican border were
deported.

The debate on the nature of the migration and the mid-1982
decision to halt deportations and to improve conditions in the camps
affected policy towards refugees in Mexico City. First, the
Guatemalans, given their vulnerability, drew the attention of those
sectors that looked favorably on the presence of Central American
refugees in Mexico. The rest of the Central Americans became secondary; and they were almost forgotten. For example, beginning in mid-

1981, there were very few news items on the presence of Central American refugees in other parts of Mexico.

Second, along with a more humanitarian policy in the camps, the authorities enforced restrictions on the entry and length of stay of other Central Americans. The permission granted to airlines to issue tourist visas to Central Americans was revoked; visas were only issued by consulates or embassies, which required evidence of economic solvency. More migration agents were sent to Chiapas. The fees for renewing migration documents were increased. And during 1983, there were daily raids against Central Americans in Mexico City.

Third, legalization became highly restrictive. For the recognized refugees it was highly selective, and almost impossible for the rest of the Central Americans. The first requests for legal permission to stay in the country were presented by the UNHCR to the Office of Migratory Affairs. Three possible outcomes resulted in these cases: a) rejection of the request, because the minimum requirements established by law were not been met; b) declaration that the matter is pending when the person making the request did not appear on the required dates; c) a granting of some type of migratory status, either political asylum (FM10) or, on a temporary basis, visitor's visa with work permit (FM3) or a student visa (FM9).

In theory, the refugees are treated like any other foreigners; but in fact, certain exceptional criteria have also been used. First, exceptions have been made when the UNHCR presents cases of undocumented persons even though the General Law on Population requires a foreigner to have a valid visa in order to prior to requesting a change of status. Second, on occasion the authorities have not applied all the requirements for obtaining a visa based on political criteria.

For example, to apply for the FM3, one must have secured employment at a high salary, depending on the number of dependents, and such employment must not displace Mexican labor. The employer must present a letter offering the job and noting the salary, in addition to a series of documents showing certification of the employer's firm with the national tax authorities and other offices. Permission is needed to change jobs. At certain times this visa was granted without taking into account the criteria of competitiveness with Mexican labor or the minimum wage requirement. In addition, the productive projects endorsed by the UNHCR have been considered equivalent to employment.

Until 1983 this system worked relatively well, albeit with delays. Since then, the number of pending cases has increased, fewer migrants have obtained legal status, and since 1984, recognition of political asylum (FM10) has been reserved for those requesting diplomatic asylum abroad.

In 1984, COMAR began to focus on the camps in the Yucatán Peninsula and suspended its programs for assisting urban refugees. The UNHCR halted its cooperation with nongovernmental organizations, and the Mexican government defined a dual policy for handling refugees in Mexico. On the one hand, the only publicly recognized refugees were the Guatemalans in the camps of Chiapas, Campeche and Quintana Roo. The residents there received UNHCR recognition and permits for temporary stay and assistance. The productive projects in the relocation camps in Campeche and Quintana Roo were particularly publicized to tout Mexico's generosity towards the refugees.

However, the other Central Americans are dispersed. Those recognized by the UNHCR in Mexico City receive a minimal level of protection, which is basically a guarantee against forced return. The rest, however, are considered economic migrants. The vast majority, recognized or not, lack documentation granting them legal residence in the country. The few Central Americans who are documented find themselves in a precarious legal situation; their migration papers are temporary (valid for three to six months) and depend on constantly-changing discretional criteria.

In our 1988 survey, about half of the 55 Central Americans interviewed at the assistance offices of the UNHCR had been recognized as refugees by that organization, as had only 18 of the 98 interviewed at PARCA, although one-half had requested recognition. The low percentage of Central Americans recognized as refugees at PARCA might perhaps be explained by a combination of factors: a) many Central Americans do not seek recognition as refugees due to lack of information or distrust; b) the criteria for obtaining recognition as illustrated in Table 16, are rigid; and, c) the vast majority of the recognized refugees-- 4,804 cases in 1987-- do not turn to nongovernmental organizations for assistance, as they receive what they need from the UNHCR assistance office.[49]   In the sample, the

TABLE 16

Population Requesting and Recognized as Refugees by UNHCR

	Total	Salvadoran	Guatemalan	Honduran	Nicaraguan
1985					
Persons requesting	943	620	185	109	29
Percentage recognized	45.2	46.7	60.0	11.9	24.1
1986					
Persons requesting	820	508	158	44	110
Percentage recognized	25.1	26.1	28.4	34.1	8.1
1987					
Persons requesting	914	515	101	46	252
Percentage recognized	25.1	33.2	45.1	41.3	36.9

Source: UNHCR. Protection Annual Report. 1985, 1986, and 1987.
(Data not available by nationality for previous years.)

majority of those interviewed at UNHCR said that at present their only sources of income were work and assistance from UNHCR. Only two percent said they had turned to other agencies for assistance after gaining recognition.

Of the Central Americans recognized as refugees by the UNHCR, 44 percent have some migratory status (17 percent political asylees (FM10); 16 percent visitors with work permits (FM3); 6 percent tourists (FMT); 4 percent students (FM9); and 1 percent immigrants with work permits (FM2). The rest of those recognized as refugees did not have papers, but 23 percent of the total was subject to a control mechanism created by the General Office of Migratory Affairs (see Table 17). This mechanism, which was in effect between 1986 and 1988, stipulated that the refugees recognized by the UNHCR who did not have documents or who had not initiated efforts to legalize their status had to go to the Office once a month to sign an immigration control list. The refugees acquired no rights, nor did they improve their chances of legalization by complying with this requirement. Nonetheless, according to statements of the director of this office, this system could be considered the initiation of a legalization process.[50]

Of those Central Americans who were not recognized by the UNHCR, either because they were turned down or simply had not approached UNHCR, only 7 percent had some migratory status (5 percent as tourists, 1 percent as political asylees, and 1 percent as students). The rest had no legal status.

It would be useful to calculate the ratio of legal-to-undocumented Central Americans. However, the lack of information and figures renders this task practically impossible. I will cite some figures simply to illustrate that the vast majority of migrants are in Mexico illegally. The UNHCR office in Mexico City estimated in 1983 that there were 120,000 Salvadorans in Mexico. This figure covers only those who could be considered refugees, and not displaced persons or other migrants. Of these, 4,804 cases resulted in recognition as refugees by 1987 (approximately 11,000 people) (i.e., roughly 10 percent of the total number of Salvadoran refugees in Mexico estimated by the same international organization.) According to the survey results, only 40 percent of the recognized refugees who turned to the UNHCR assistance offices have some document accrediting their legal stay in the country.

TABLE 17

Current Documentation Status of Central Americans Interviewed

Recognized Refugees

Documents	El Salvador n= 46	Guatemala n= 13	Honduras n= 8	Nicaragua n= 2	Total n= 69	%
FM2	---	1	---	---	1	1.4
FM3	8	3	---	---	11	15.9
FM9	1	2	---	---	3	4.3
FM10	6	1	5	---	12	17.4
FMT	3	---	1	---	4	5.8
Control	13	2	---	1	16	23.2
Undocumented	15	4	2	1	22	31.9
Illegals %	60.9	46.2	25.0	100.0	---	
Visas W/P %	30.4	38.5	62.5	---	---	

Not recognized

Documents	n= 64	n= 18	n= 1	n= 1	n= 84	%
FM9	1	---	---	---	1	1.2
FM10	1	---	---	---	1	1.2
FMT	3	1	---	---	4	4.8
Control	1	---	---	---	1	1.2
Undocumented	58	17	1	1	77	91.7
Illegals %	92.2	94.4	100.0	100.0	---	
Visa W/P %	1.6	---	---	---	---	

Source: Survey of 153 Central Americans, 1988

Visas W/P: Visas with work permit (FM2, FM3, and FM10)
Control: Monthly control of signatures
Illegals: People without migratory documents, this figure is equivalent to the sum of the undocumented and those monitored under the signature control mechanism.

The lack of immigration papers and refugee status has led to insecurity and difficulty in integration. The refugees not only have run the risk of deportation, but also have failed to receive the individual guarantees that the Mexican Constitution establishes for every person in its territory. For example, the Constitution stipulates that all persons born in the country have the right to Mexican nationality. Nonetheless, the administrative requirements for registering newborns have made it difficult for Central Americans to do so, and other requirements have made it difficult for them to gain access to education and public health.

In the case of Central American families with school-age children, a wide range of factors have affected the decision to send the children to school: the value they place on education; economic resources available; and contacts that help them register children without legal papers. As illustrated in Table 18, a larger percentage of Central Americans recognized as refugees send their children to school than those without such recognition.

TABLE 18

Access to Education

	Salvadorans		Guatemalans	
	RE	NR	RE	NR
Families with School-Age Children	43.5	31.3	53.8	33.3
School Attendance (as percentage of families with school-age children)	90.0	75.0	57.1	33.3

Source: Survey of 153 Central Americans, 1988
RE: Recognized
NR: Not recognized

LABOR MARKET PARTICIPATION

Finding paid work without documents is quite difficult. Being illegal in a city profoundly struck by the economic crisis makes it impossible to find a permanent, well-paid job. In 1980, the official unemployment rate in the city was 15 percent of the economically active population, and 30 percent for those who would want to work, but who at the time of the survey were not looking.

According to our survey results, 43.4 percent of the Central Americans were unemployed when interviewed at the UNHCR and PARCA. Although the lack of job opportunities is no doubt a fundamental problem for the migrants, this figure may overestimate the unemployment rate for Central Americans as a whole. In fact, as noted in the section on the role of nongovernmental organizations, the population turns to the agencies largely to seek economic support for survival when there is little or no work.

For example, beginning in 1984, only one-third of the Central Americans recognized as refugees had requested assistance from the UNHCR offices. Assistance has consisted of a "subsistence allowance" granted to the unemployed no more than four times during the first year of their stay in Mexico City, scholarships, assistance for covering costs of getting settled and for medical services, or assistance to retirees and groups considered vulnerable. Nonetheless, 60 percent of those who requested assistance in the first quarter of 1989 received it either because they were unemployed or could not cover an emergency expense.[51]

Those who were employed at the time of the interview worked in a wide array of activities. Forty-three percent worked in services: domestic work and child care; as drivers and mechanics; and as secretaries and employees of small offices and workshops. The second largest occupational category is construction: 6 percent work as stone masons, painters, and plasterers. The third largest category

of migrants work in petty commerce, mainly as street vendors and
newspaper sellers.

The unemployment rate of the population interviewed
depends to a great extent on their occupational sector in the country
of origin. Unemployment is highest among the 20 percent of migrants
from the agricultural sector. At the time of the interview 68 percent of
the migrants had no job, while the rest had found work in the service
sector (17 percent), construction (7 percent), or small-scale commerce (3 percent). Forty-four percent of those who had worked in
construction in Central America (which is 12 percent of the total)
were unemployed at the time of the survey. The rest worked in services (27 percent), construction (17 percent) and manufacturing and
commerce (6 percent each).

Unemployment among those who worked in the service sec-
tor in Central America (54 percent of the total interviewed) is a little
lower. Thirty-seven percent had no job at the time of the interview,
while 56 percent were working, in services in Mexico. The rest
worked in construction (4 percent) and manufacturing and small-scale
commerce (1 percent, each).

According to the survey, those who are able to enter the labor
market most easily are small-scale merchants (8 percent of the
sample) and manufacturing workers (5 percent). Seventy percent of
the small-scale merchants are employed; 70 percent of those
employed are in services and 20 percent in commerce. Seventy-one
percent of the manufacturing workers were employed; 29 percent in
services, 29 percent in manufacturing, and 14 percent in construction.

As illustrated in Table 19, the unemployment rate among in-
terviewees is related to the length of stay in Mexico. For example, all
of the peasants interviewed were unemployed for six months from the
time of their arrival. Nevertheless, among those who turned to the
agencies during their first month in Mexico City, unemployment was
68 percent. Of those who do so from the first to sixth month, 56 percent were unemployed, and of those who were interviewed after
having been in Mexico City for six months, 32 percent were unemployed.

In addition to the high unemployment rate, working conditi-
tions are difficult for migrants. Of those who were working when interviewed, 72 percent worked in the informal sector, in part-time jobs

TABLE 19

Unemployment Rate by Length of Stay in Mexico City

	Time in Mexico City								
	Less than 1 month			1 to 6 months			More than 6 months		
	Total	Unemp.	%	Total	Unemp.	%	Total	Unemp.	%
	n= 19	n= 13	68.4	n= 39	n= 22	56.4	n= 93	n= 30	32.4
Agricultural	7	7	100.0	8	8	100.0	15	6	40.0
Manufacturing	0	0	0.0	2	0	0.0	4	1	25.0
Small Commerce	1	1	100.0	4	1	25.0	7	2	28.5
Construction	2	0	0.0	6	2	33.3	11	6	54.4
Services	9	5	55.5	18	11	61.1	55	14	25.4
Others	-	-	--	1	0	0.0	1	1	100.0

Source: Survey of 153 Central Americans

without contracts, benefits, or minimum wages. Fifty-one percent earned less than the legal minimum wage, and 32 percent had jobs that paid the minimum wage. On average, the wages varied by economic sector (see Table 20). Those who worked in agriculture, manufacturing, and small commerce averaged less than the legal minimum wage. Those who worked in construction and services earned on average the legal minimum wage.

Interestingly, the unemployment rate and the wage level do not vary between the population accorded refugee status and those without UNHCR recognition. Although the unemployment rate is logically less -- 35 percent -- among the population with work permits (FM3 and FM2) than among the undocumented migrants, their working conditions are no better. Only 8 percent of those interviewed had work permits.

A major change in the employment situation of the family takes place in Mexico City. Whereas in the place of origin more than one-third of the families had at least two people working, in Mexico City there is only one wage earner in 90 percent of the cases.

Over one-half of the migrants interviewed consider the unstable labor situation to be the main problem they face in Mexico City (see Table 21). This figure may overestimate the importance of the labor problem because only persons who sought assistance were interviewed. Nevertheless, it is an indicator of the population's precarious living conditions: insecurity, shortages, and overcrowded living conditions, lack of services, and malnutrition.

TABLE 20

Wage by Sector in Month Prior to Interview

	Less than Min. Wage	One Min. Wage	1-2 Min. Wage	2 Min. Wage	Total
Agriculture	2				2
Manufacturing	2	1			3
Small Commerce	4	1			5
Construction	4	3	2		9
Services	21	16	6	3	46
Total	33	21	8	3	65
%	50.8	32.3	12.3	4.6	

Source: Survey of 153 Central Americans, 1988

MW: base minimum wage (legal minimum wage= 259,500 monthly pesos in 1989 (just over US$100.00 per month). Salaries are calculated on multiples of the base minimum wage.

TABLE 21

Main Problems in Mexico City*

Problems	%
Lack of employment	46.8
Lack of services	44.7
Poor economic situation	22.4
Insecurity due to illegal status	22.3
Poor diet	14.6
Xenophobia	4.8
Expensive rent	4.0
Poorly paid work	2.0

Source: Survey of 153 Central Americans

*Individuals responded more than once

PROSPECTS FOR RETURN

Despite isolation, insecure legal status, legal and administrative problems, lack of services, and unemployment experienced by newly arrived Central Americans in the Mexican capital and other major cities, migration has persisted as a permanent phenomenon. The conditions that led to massive migration still prevail, and in some cases have gotten worse; peace in Central America is still far-off.

Moreover, return is conditioned by each migrant's assessment of the advantages and drawbacks of remaining in Mexico, returning home, or continuing north. In order to return, migrants must be certain that their personal safety and that of their families would be guaranteed in their country of origin; they must also feel assured of finding acceptable economic conditions (see Table 22). For some, being able to participate in politics is fundamental. While Central Americans in Mexico City would like to not feel like foreigners, and to be able to reembrace their own culture, the city does offer certain advantages, such as greater expectations for education and access to services; large markets for goods and labor; and in many cases, better wages.

To date, only those Central Americans who are relatively concentrated-- in the refugee camps in Mexico and Honduras-- have seriously considered returning. They seek to repatriate in groups, and in an organized manner. This has occurred among Nicaraguans in Honduran Mosquitia and, to some extent among the Salvadorans at Mesa Grande. Returning as a group gives them greater leverage to negotiate, enhances their security, and improves their possibilities of obtaining better economic conditions-- access to land and the means of production.[52]

Government of those nations most affected by the population displacement (Guatemala, El Salvador, and Nicaragua) have also negotiated with "interested countries" (West Germany, France, The

TABLE 22

Necessary Conditions for Returning

	El Salvador n= 110	Guatemala n= 31	Honduras n= 9	Nicaragua n= 3
Improved economic situation	11.8	6.4	--	--
Change in government	15.4	29.0	30.0	--
End of repression	31.8	32.2	55.5	--
Guarantee of security	28.1	32.2	11.1	--
Other	39.9	41.9	11.1	66.6
No response	10.0	3.2	--	33.3

Source: Survey of 153 Central Americans, 1983

* Individuals responded more than once

Netherlands, Italy, Norway, Sweden, and the European Community)
to obtain development funds for regions in which repatriation may
take place.[53]

      For the Central Americans in Mexico City, who are from a
great many places and a wide variety of social sectors, and who live in
relative isolation, returning in this fashion is not realistic. Therefore,
returning safely and regaining what has been lost is a remote possibility. According to the survey results, repatriation is considered by
a minority. Only 32 percent of the Salvadorans and 13 percent of the
Guatemalans intend to return, and not in the short term (see
Table 23).

TABLE 23

Short and Long-Term Plans by Nationality*

	El Salvador n= 110		Guatemala n= 31	
	Short-term	Long-term	Short-term	Long-term
Establish themselves in Mexico City	31.8	17.3	58.1	22.6
Go to another city	1.8	1.8	---	3.2
Return	21.8	31.8	6.5	12.9
Go to another country	39.1	33.6	25.8	32.3
Other	2.7	1.8	---	3.2
No response	2.7	13.6	9.7	25.8

Sources: Survey of 153 Central Americans, 1988

*For current purposes, under three years is considered "short-term," anything greater, long-term

CONCLUSIONS

The population displacements in Central America that have resulted from social conflicts are a complex and highly varied phenomena. One way to understand it better is to study those who migrate in small groups and become integrated to varying degrees among the local population. This study of Central American migration to Mexico City provides some information on the dynamics of migration. Nonetheless, it should be considered a preliminary assessment of the phenomenon. To date, no other studies on this subject have been published, and the results of our study offer more questions than answers. Issues such as the profile of the migrant population and its change over time, the organization of Central Americans in the city, the impact of Mexican society, and the long-term consequences on the migrants' places of origin should be examined in greater depth.

Likewise, the demographic characteristics and expectations of Nicaraguan migrants needs attention. Few Nicaraguans took part in this survey which underestimated their presence in Mexico City. Since the Nicaraguans have been excluded from the aid programs of most of the nongovernmental organizations, their living conditions and patterns of integration should be compared with those of other Central Americans who enjoy greater assistance. Such a comparison might indicate the importance of the assistance agencies in the migrants' daily lives.

The impact of the restrictive immigration policies of the United States and Canada on the number of Central Americans in Mexico City is a key issue that deserves further attention.

The first conclusion of this study is that the massive presence of Central Americans in Mexico City is unprecedented. In the past migration was limited to a small number of students, professionals, and political leaders. At present the number of migrants and their rate of growth are on the rise. The demographic profile of the migrants has changed; and over the years the gradual increase in the number of women and dependents distinguish this migration from the economically motivated migrations of undocumented persons. The demographic profile of these migrants is similar to that of legal migrants and of migration involving the displacement of entire populations, such as results from natural disasters and armed conflicts. These, the migrants are from a variety of social backgrounds. Professionals and university students account for a small part of the total. Urban migrants from the service and construction sectors are the most typical, although there are now considerable number of migrants from semi-urban and rural areas.

Second, we conclude that a number of factors determine the place of arrival and act to filter the migrants who arrive in Mexico City. These include age and number of children or dependents, educational level, social and geographic background, and networks for exchange and reception. In this regard, those who have been displaced by conflict cannot adhere to a logic that is radically different from that of other migrants. In fact, they use traditional migratory routes and social networks of exchange and reception. As with other migrations, contacts in the place of destination is a determining factor behind the decision to migrate. In the case of Central Americans fleeing the conflicts, networks of family ties, which are typical of economic migrations, are complemented by the nongovernmental organizations, and the churches. There is an expectation that they will be welcomed upon their arrival. Furthermore, the choice of destination depends on the possibility of finding work and being able to pass undetected.

In this sense, research that has centered on analyzing the Central Americans' motives for departure, whether in surveys or studies of the conditions of violence and repression in the place of origin, illustrate the political nature of this migration, but do not help us understand the dynamics of the actual displacement. Furthermore, the arguments that migrants use to justify their migration do not always reflect the complexity of this phenomenon.

Third, although the present volume of Central American migration to Mexico City is large in comparison to pre-1978 migration and to the total number of persons displaced by the conflicts in Central America; nonetheless, it is a minor phenomenon in proportion to the level migration of Mexicans to Mexico City, as well as in proportion to the city's total population. The Central Americans mix in with the residents of the capital and become lost in the crowd. The impact of the migration may be greater in the places of origin. According to the results of this study, the population that migrates to Mexico City has received higher levels of education and more economic resources that those who migrate closer to home. Professionals, of whom there are relatively few in the region, have migrated en masse to far-away destinations abroad, and it is unlikely that they will return, considering the time they have spent abroad, the persistence of the conflicts, the ongoing economic deterioration, the bleak outlook for reintegration in their place of origin, and the expectations generated by Mexico City.

Finally, the presence of Central Americans in Mexico City and throughout the metropolitan area is not a short-term phenomenon, and it is foreseeable that their numbers will grow in coming years. The measures taken by the Mexican government to slow down the entry and shorten stay of Central Americans -- increased surveillance along the southern border, migration check points, raids, and restrictions on legal entry and subsequent legalization -- have not stopped the flow or reduced the number of Central Americans in the country, though they have increased the costs of migration. However, such measures have increased the number of migrants without legal status. For the migrants this means insecurity, social and occupational problems, less access to services, and the loss of state control over the foreigners. The tendency of the Mexican authorities to ignore the political origin of the migratory phenomenon and their refusal to establish mechanisms for effective protection has placed those migrants who fear for their lives or liberty in their home countries in a highly vulnerable situation, in which they are subject to deportation. This situation jeopardizes Mexico's tradition of asylum. Moreover, the Mexican government has limited the total volume of international resources available to assist the Central Americans. The Central American presence is a long-term phenomenon affecting the entire region, which will not be substantially changed by administrative measures or xenophobic attitudes.

It is important, or at least desirable, that those who play a role in the migrants' lives--authorities, nongovernmental organizations, and international agencies--should see in the Central American population in Mexico City not a source of problems, but an opportunity to expand their horizons and share with them the history and cultural wealth of the Central American peoples.

Notes

1. Sergio Aguayo and Patricia Weiss Fagen, *Central Americans in Mexico and the United States* (Washington, DC: Hemispheric Migration Project. Center for Immigration Policy and Refugee Assistance. Georgetown University, 1988), Appendix.

2. By Mexico City, I mean the 16 political delegations of the urban area in the Federal District, and the municipalities of the state of Mexico that lie in the metropolitan area, namely: Atizapán de Zaragoza, Coacoalco, Cuautitlán Izcalli, Chalco, Chicoloapan, Chimalhuacán, Ecatepec, Huixquilucan, Ixtapalapa, Naucalpan, Netzahuacóyotl, Nicolás Romero, La Paz, Tecámac, Tlanepantla, and Tultitán. This definition corresponds to that used by the Departamento del Distrito Federal (government of the Federal District). See, Departamento del Distrito Federal and El Colegio de Mexico. *Atlas de la Ciudad de Mexico*. 1987.

3. Lars Schoultz, "Central America," The University of North Carolina. (January 1987):7-8. mimeo.

4. For a brief analysis of the literature see Laura O'Dogherty, "The Hidden Face of the War in Central America," *Current Sociology* 36, 2(1988):93-106.

5. A detailed description of the assumptions behind the migration theory based on push and pull factors may be consulted in: Alejandro Portes and Robert Bach, *Latin Journey, Cuban and Mexican Immigrants in the United States*. (Berkeley and Los Angeles: University of California Press, 1985); and Robert Bach, *Western Hemispheric Immigration to the United States: A Review of Selected Research Trends*. (Washington, DC: Hemispheric Migration Project, Center for Immigration Policy and Refugee Assistance Georgetown University, 1985), 110.

6. The sample size for the population from UNHCR and PARCA is determined by the formula $n = No^2/(N-1)D + o^2$ with $D = B^2/4$, where o^2 is the population variance, N represents the population count and B is the margin of error. Given the dispersion of the population studied and the lack of data on their characteristics, the sample had to be designed estimating N and o^2. Data from the population requesting assistance from either of the institutions in 1987 was used for designing the sample. For N, we took the number of cases requesting assistance by nationality in 1987, and the population variance for both institutions was calculated on the basis of the variance in the ages of those seeking assistance.

7. The Program to Assist Central American Refugees (PARCA) was chosen to administer the survey, since it has been the nongovernmental agency to which the largest number of Central Americans have turned, and it has come to be rather well-known. In this sense, the data for population attended by PARCA since 1985 could be representative of the Central American population requesting assistance, with the exception of Nicaraguans who were excluded from this assistance. PARCA was founded in September 1980 within the American Friends Service Committee to assist the Central American population. Beginning in July 1983, it became part of Servicio, Desarrollo y Paz. Its activities have primarily involved promoting awareness in Mexico of migrants' rights and assisting the population by providing emergency aid and primary health care services.

8. Carlos Zazueta and Luis Pablos, *Migrantes Centroamericanos en Mexico: Primer Informe Preliminar de Trabajadores Centroamericanos a la República Mexicana*, (Mexico: CENIET, 1982), 32.

9. Ibid., 32-40.

10. Linda S. Peterson, *Central American Migration: Past and Present* (Washington DC: Center for International Research. U.S. Bureau of the Census, 1986), 47; and UNHCR, "Number of Refugees as of 31 March 1987 in the Northern Latin American Countries covered by R.O. San José, B.O. Mexico City, and B.O. Tegucigalpa."

11. International Council of Voluntary Agencies, Consultation, Geneva, 1986.

12. *Diario Oficial*, July 22, 1980.

13. Comisión Mexicana de Ayuda a Refugiados, Area de Trabajo Social, Reports of May and November 1981, and January to December of 1983.

14. Data provided by the Programa de Estudios de Refugiados (PARCA).

15. COMAR, Area de Trabajo Social, documents cited.

16. Americas Watch, *Guatemalan Refugees in Mexico: 1980-1984*, (Washington, DC: America's Watch Committee, 1984) and Intergovernmental Committee for Migration (ICM), *Guatemalan and Salvadoran Refugees in Mexico* (Geneva: Hemispheric Migration Project, ICM, 1984), cited in Peterson, *op. cit.*, 45.

17. United Nations High Commissioner for Refugees, "Number of Refugees as of 31 March 1987," Geneva, 1987.

18. ICVA, *op. cit.*

19. According to Gilda Larios, who worked with PARCA from its founding in 1980 until 1984, and Rafael González Franco, coordinator of the program from 1985 to date, from the outset Nicaraguans were not considered as beneficiaries of the program. This criterion was first set forth explicitly in the 1986 report, as the number of Nicaraguans seeking assistance increased. SEDEPAC, PARCA. "Informe de Actividades," October 11, 1986.

20. UNHCR. "Report on Protection Activities," 1986, 1987.

21. Interview with Gilda Larios.

22. Zazueta and Pablos, *op. cit.*, 58.

23. COMAR. "Informe estadístico de la Oficina de Trabajo Social," September, October, November, and December 1983.

24. Sergio Aguayo, *El Exodo Centroamericano* (Mexico City: SEP, 1986), and Sergio Aguayo and Patricia Weiss Fagen, *Central Americans in Mexico and the United States* (Washington, DC: Hemispheric Migration Project, Center for Immigration Policy and Refugee Assistance, Georgetown University, 1988).

25. In the daily papers of El Salvador (*La Prensa, Gráfica* and *El Diario de Hoy*) and Guatemala (*La Prensa*) classified ads offer travel services for people wanting to go to Mexico City, Tijuana, and any point in the United States, "safe, with no need for documents." On occasion, travellers are offered service directly to the doorstep, paying on arrival at the destination. For example, in the Guatemalan daily *La Prensa* (January 11, 1989) there are ads announcing "Daily excursions. Priority for Nicaraguans. We offer safety and responsibility in travel to the United States, Mexico...."

26. The Central Americans interviewed, especially Salvadorans, stated that their choice of Mexico City as their destination was determined in part by their knowledge of and familiarity with the city, Mexico's tradition of asylum, and the impact of the Franco-Mexican Declaration of 1981 in support of the Farabundo Martí National Liberation Front.

27. Carlos Zazueta and García Griego, *Encuesta Nacional de Emigración a la Frontera Norte del País y a los Estados Unidos* (Mexico: CENIET, 1978-1979); and U.S. Department of Justice, Immigration and Naturalization Service, *Annual Report* (Washington, DC: INS, 1977), cited by Zazueta and Pablos, *op. cit.*, 15.

28. Zazueta and Pablos, *op. cit.*, 14.

29. See Francisco Alba Hernández, "Exodo silencioso: la inmigración de trabajadores mexicanos a Estados Unidos," in *Foro Internacional* 66, 17 (1976):153-172; Juan Ruiz Diez-Canedo, *La migración indocumentada a Estados Unidos: un nuevo enfoque* (Mexico City: FCE, 1984); Carlos Zazueta and García Griego, *Los Trabajadores Mexicanos en Estados Unidos, Resultados de la Encuesta Nacional de Emigración a la Frontera Norte del Pais y a los Estados Unidos* (Mexico: CENIET, 1978 and 1979), and El Colegio de Mexico, *Indocumentados: mitos y realidades* (Mexico: El Colegio de Mexico, 1979).

30. Universidad Centroamericana "José Simeón Cañas,(UCA)" *Desplazados y Refugiados.* Informe Preliminar (El Salvador, 1985), 193-199. The text draws on results of a survey done by the UCA in 1984 of the displaced dispersed within El Salvador (315 families surveyed), and the dispersed refugees in Costa Rica (25 families) and Nicaragua (28 families).

31. See Sergio Aguayo and Laura O'Dogherty, "Refugiados Guatemaltecos en Campeche y Quintana Roo," *Foro Internacional* XXVII, 106 (1986): 266-295; and Segundo Montes, "La Situación de los Salvadoreños Desplazados y Refugiados," *Estudios Centroamericanos* XXIX, 434, (San Salvador, 1984): 904-920.

32. Jorge B. Arias, *La población de Guatemala* (Guatemala City: Instituto Centroamericano de Investigación y Tecnología Industrial and Universidad del Valle, Guatemala City, 1976) 35-37.

33. UCA, *op. cit.*, 32.

34. Jorge B. Arias, *op. cit.*, 53 (data on Guatemala), and UCA, 1985, *op. cit.*, p. 20 (data on El Salvador).

35. Segúndo Montes Mozo with Juan José García Vásquez, *Salvadoran Migration to the United States: An Exploratory Study* (Washington, DC: Hemispheric Migration Project, Center for Immigration Policy and Refugee Assistance, Georgetown University, 1988), 21.

36. Virgilio Partida Bush, "El proceso de migración a la ciudad de mexico," in *Atlas de la Ciudad de Mexico*, Departamento del Distrito Federal and El Colegio de Mexico (1987) 134-139.

37. See Lourdes Arizpe, "La migración por relevos y la reproducción social del campesinado," in *Cuadernos del CES 28,* (Centro de Estudios Sociológicos, El Colegio de Mexico, 1980); Wayne Cornelius, *Los Inmigrantes pobres en la Ciudad de Mexico y la política* (Mexico City: FCE, 1980; and Larissa Lomitz, *Cómo sobreviven los marginados* (Mexico City: Siglo XXI, 1985).

38. See René Herrera and Mario Ojeda, "La Política de Mexico hacia Centroamérica, 1979-1982," *Jornadas* (Mexico: El Colegio de Mexico)103 (1983).

39. Since 1979 Christian groups, solidarity groups, and leftist parties in Mexico City have spoken out on significant events in Central American politics, mainly the Sandinista victory and the assassination of Msgr. Romero in El Salvador. For example, in April 1980, Christian groups and leftist parties marched to the Basilica of Guadalupe to protest the assassination of Msgr. Romero (*Proceso,* 179, April 1980). In 1981 the National Coordinating Committee of the Popular Urban Movement (CONAMUP) organized the First International Meeting of the Popular Urban Movement in solidarity with the Salvadoran revolution. It participated in establishing the World Front for Solidarity with the Salvadoran People, and established contacts with the Committee in Solidarity with the Guatemalan People. However, beginning in 1982, CONAMUP relegated solidarity activities to a secondary level. According to Ramírez Sainz, a student of the popular urban movement, the efforts of the National Coordinating Committee are focused on negotiations with the Federal District government, and participating in the National Front to Defend Wages Against the Austerity Program and Shortages [Juan Manuel Ramírez, *El Movimiento Urbano Popular en Mexico* (Mexico City: Siglo XXI, 1986) 191]. A similar process occurred with the Christian Base Communities. The national scene has become more important. In about 1984, enthusiasm began to decline. By 1988, for example, the Christian Base Communities agreed not to organize more than one activity to commemorate the anniversary of the Sandinista Revolution, so as to focus their energies on the work with grass-roots organizations in Mexico and their internal problems. The commemoration of Romero's death, is still celebrated every April, but with fewer participants.

40. Central Americans in Mexico City are able to request resettlement in a third country, usually Canada or Australia. As set forth in its 1984 Annual Protection Report, the UNHCR established a restrictive policy that authorizes resettlement only in special cases because of the lack of opportunities. In 1987, for example, 108 family groups were settled under UNHCR auspices: 78 from El Salvador, 10 from Guatemala, 19 from Nicaragua, and 1 from Honduras. To qualify for resettlement in a third country, refugees must: a) not have their safety guaranteed in Mexico, either because of persecution there, or because the authorities will not allow them to stay there;

b) have humanitarian needs, relating to age or physical condition; or
c) request and obtain a work permit and visa from the country of destination. This last case is dependent on the immigration programs in
the country of destination, which generally favor Central Americans
with greater technical qualifications. The Canadian embassy in
Mexico City has an immigration program for Central Americans that
offers migration opportunities for small groups. To be accepted one
must be young and healthy, have technical skills, and travel without
elderly relatives. Those who have taken college courses or have
degrees must renounce in writing their rights to any future academic
revalidation of their degrees. In 1986 the Canadian immigration service reduced the annual migration quota by 50 percent (at present 700
persons are accepted annually); beginning in 1987, those wishing to
participate in this program have had to be recognized as refugees by
the UNHCR, and the processing delay may last as long as a year.

41. Migrants are generally classified as "political" or
"economic." Nonetheless, it is increasingly clear that in situations of
generalized conflict, such as that of the Central American region, the
distinction between the two categories becomes blurred. For example, a survey in El Salvador showed that, as migrants see it,
economic and political conditions appear to be linked. In the survey,
it is particularly revealing that in determining whether there was a
relationship between the worsening economic outlook and a decline in
the respect for life, 75.6 percent of those surveyed stated that employment conditions are poor or very poor, 75.7 percent stated that
respect for life is also poor or very poor. (Instituto de Derechos
Humanos [IDHUCA], Universidad Centroamericana "José Simeón
Cañas," La resistencia no violenta ante los regímenes salvadoreños
que han utilizado el terror institucionalizado en el período 1972-1987,"
San Salvador, 1988.)

42. According to the work of Al Hester, "Three Mexico City
Tabloid Newspapers: Some Surprises." *Studies in Latin American
Popular Culture* 4 (1985): 111-121, the largest circulation newspapers
in Mexico City, excluding those dedicated to sports, are: *La Prensa*,
daily circulation 278,000 (12.1% of the total); the afternoon edition of
Ovaciones, 228,000 (9.9%); and the morning edition of *Ovaciones,*
203,000 (8.8%). In *La Prensa*, for example, 11.3% of the articles are
crime reports, preceded by articles on domestic politics (30%) and
sports coverage (13.8%). See also, David G. LaFrance, "A Survey of
Mexico City Newspapers." *Studies in Latin American Popular Culture,*
4 (1985): 97-110; and "Aproximación al estudio de la prensa diaria

mexicana," *Revista Mexicana de Ciencias Políticas*, 23 (Oct.- Dec. 1976 to January-March 1977):86-87, 271-300.

43. *Ovaciones,* 2nd edition, January 19, 1987.

Other articles along the same lines:

"Salvadorans were identified as those who robbed the Banco Comermex, according to one of the assailants...who added that the rest of the band is hiding out in Ciudad Netzahualcóyotl." (*Ovaciones*, 2nd edition, March 31, 1988); "Much of the crime, drugs, and prostitution from which we suffer has been imported from countries to the south." (*Ovaciones*, 2nd edition, January 20, 1987); "Band of foreign assailants (Salvadorans and Guatemalans) arrested... With this arrest it is clear that the metropolitan area, and various parts of the country in general, have come to be preferred by foreigners for international crime ... it is clear that international thieves enter and leave this country,as if they were in their own home,' in addition to considering Mexico a paradise for thievery because of the facilities available to them here, the lack of security and the inability of the police to protect the citizenry." (*La Prensa*, October 17, 1986); "Three grenades go off in Ciudad Hidalgo, attributed to protesters, gamblers, and illegal Central Americans" (*La Prensa*, February 2, 1986); "Dressed as guerrillas, a band of Salvadorans carried out more than 300 robberies. A group of Salvadorans who entered our country illegally committed some 300 robberies during the course of several years, with assistance from some Mexicans....They were arrested by the Judicial police. Their hideout was in Ajusco....Investigations show that there are Central Americans of other nationalities organized to commit crimes in our country." (*Ovaciones*, 2nd edition, June 1985).

44. *La Prensa*, January 28, 1986.

Other articles:

"Central Americans flee. They threaten to enter our country as illegal aliens....An undetermined quantity of Central and South American citizens could enter Mexico using false documents and counterfeit passports" (*Ovaciones*, 2nd edition, March 18, 1988); "Having no strategy or policy for follow-up, plagued by administrative disorder and obsolete methods as well as corruption and negligence, our immigration services have facilitated this invasion, which has brought us not only serious economic problems, but social ones as well. The invasion is such that we are threatened by all types of undesirable foreigners, as can be seen in the Zona Rosa and other parts of the city, such as in the arcades downtown, where musical groups play folk music" (*Ovaciones*, 2nd edition, January 21, 1987).

The case of an illegal urban settlement in the southern part of the city (in the Lomas del Seminario District in Ajusco), that ended in the eviction of the squatters in December 1988, was widely linked to Central Americans in press and television coverage. For months prior to the eviction, for example, the magazine Revelación stated that "five thousand families, most of whom appear to be Central American refugees..., decided to settle on the foothills of Ajusco, without taking into account the infraction they were committing....It is said that there are large paramilitary training camps where they use different types of weapons of various calibers, which they apparently purchase at the U.S. border. Mixed in among the main leaders of the squatters;...are a great many 'guerrillas'" (August 15, 1988). Similar comments appear in the print and broadcast media.

45. Joan Friedland and Jesús Rodríguez y Rodríguez, *Seeking Safe Ground. The Legal Situation of Central American Refugees in Mexico* (San Diego, CA: Mexico-U.S. Law Institute, University of San Diego Law School and Instituto de Investigaciones Jurídicas, Universidad Nacional Autónoma de Mexico, 1987).

46. For a listing of international and regional treaties and declarations, resolutions of the United Nations General Assembly, domestic legislation, and ad hoc agreements on asylum and refuge in Mexico, see Laura O'Dogherty, "Algunos documentos relativos al asilo y refugio en Mexico, Documentos del Coloquio sobre el Derecho de Asilo," El Colegio de Mexico and the Academia Mexicana de Derechos Humanos, Mexico, June 1985.

47. In the General Provisions of the Annex to the Statute of the Office of the United Nations High Commissioner for Refugees, it is stated that UNHCR, "acting under the authority of the General Assembly, shall assume the function of providing international protection, under the auspices of the United Nations, to refugees who fall within the scope of the present Statute and of seeking permanent solutions for the problem of refugees by assisting governments and, subject to the approval of the governments concerned, private organizations to facilitate the voluntary repatriation of such refugees, or their assimilation within new national communities."

48. Agreement between the United Nations High Commissioner for Refugees and the Mexican Committee for Refugee Assistance, March 2, 1981.

49. The assistance provided by UNHCR consists of scholarships, subsistence allowances, settlement expenses, assistance to vulnerable groups (retirees, the ill, and widows and widowers with children), and support for productive projects. Those recognized as refugees have the right to attend public schools, and to use government health services. For most, the assistance provided accounts for a large percentage of their income.

50. Interview with staff in charge of protection for UNHCR refugees (June 1989) and staff of nongovernmental organizations.

51. Report of the UNHCR Assistance Office, January to March 1989; and interview with the Program Coordinator, Ana Cecilia Salgado.

52. Particularly relevant in this regard are the process of repatriations of Salvadoran refugees from Mesa Grande in Honduras, the negotiations between the Miskitos in Honduras and the Sandinista government, and the proposals of the Permanent Committees of Guatemalan refugees in Mexico.

53. The Central American governments and Mexico sponsored in May 1989 in Guatemala City, the International Conference on Central American Refugees (CIREFCA). One of its main purposes was to seek funds from the international community to reconstruct the areas affected by massive migration, and thereby facilitate repatriation. In the cases of Guatemala and El Salvador, only the regions from which the population in refugee camps originate are contemplated. In Nicaragua, the focus is on the Atlantic Coast region.

ABOUT THE AUTHOR

Laura O'Dogherty is a researcher associated with the Academia Mexicana de Derechos Humanos in Mexico City.

HEMISPHERIC MIGRATION PROJECT
Expert Review Group

Francisco Alba - El Colegio de Mexico
Patricia Anderson, Ph.D - University of the West Indies, Jamaica
Charles Keely, Ph.D - Georgetown University
Peter Marchetti, SJ - Universidad Centroamericana, Nicaragua
Lelio Mármora, Ph.D - Intergovernmental Committee for Migration, Argentina
Christopher Mitchell, Ph.D - New York University
Gabriel Murillo - Universidad de los Andes, Colombia
Alan Simmons, Ph.D - York University, Canada
Edelberto Torres-Rivas - Facultad Latinoamericana de las Ciencias Sociales, Costa Rica

---

HMP Staff

Harold Bradley, SJ - Director, CIPRA
Patricia R. Pessar, Ph.D - Research Director, CIPRA
Mary Ann Larkin - Assistant Director, HMP
Gerardo D. Berthin - Administrative Assistant, HMP

HEMISPHERIC MIGRATION PROJECT
LIST OF PUBLICATIONS

Central Americans in Mexico City: Uprooted and Silenced, Laura O'Dogherty, 1989. US $7.50.

Nicaraguan Refugees in Costa Rica: Adjustment to Camp Life, Gilda Pacheco, 1989. US $7.50.

Return in Latin America, Lelio Mármora, 1989. US $7.50.

Central American Refugees 1989. Workshop Report on Central American Refugee Research: Recommendations for Policy, April 7-8, 1989, Consejo Superior Universitario/Hemispheric Migration Project. US $7.50.

On the Farm: Migration, Smallholder Agriculture, and Food Consumption in Jamaica and Saint Lucia, West Indies, Elsa M. Chaney, 1988. US $7.50.

Salvadoran Migration to the United States: An Exploratory Study, Segundo Montes Mozo, S.J. and Juan José Garcia Vasquéz, 1988. US $7.50.

The Other Refugees: A Study of Undocumented Guatemalans in Chiapas, Mexico, Luis Raúl Salvadó, 1988. US $7.50.

When Borders Don't Divide: Labor Migration and Refugee Movements in the Americas, Patricia R. Pessar, editor, 1988. Order from Center for Migration Studies, (Order directly from CMS. ATTN: Ann Munafo, 209 Flagg Place, Staten Island, NY 10304-1199. (718) 351-8800).

Migration, War, and Agrarian Reform: The Peasant Settlements in Nicaragua, Jon Ander Bilbao E., 1988. US $7.50.

Central Americans in Mexico and the United States, Sergio Aguayo and Patricia Weiss Fagen, 1988. *(Sold out)*

Repatriation and Reintegration: An Arduous Process in Guatemala, Beatriz Manz, 1988. US $7.50.

Return to Rio de la Plata: Response to the Return of Exiles in Argentina and Uruguay, Lelio Mármora, 1988. US $7.50.

The New U.S. Immigration Law: It Impact on Jamaicans at Home and Abroad, Patricia Y. Anderson, 1988. US $5.00.

The Immigration Reform and Control Act: Implications for Colombia and Colombians in the United States, Political Science Department, Universidad de los Andes, Bogotá, 1988. US $5.00.

Proceedings of the Inter-American Conference on Migration Trends and Policies, February 4-6, 1986, Mary Ann Larkin, editor. 1987 US $7.50. (Also in Spanish translation).

Western Hemisphere Migration to the U.S., Robert Bach, 1985. US $5.00.

International Migration in the Southern Cone, Jorge Balan, 1985. US $5.00.

Migration from the Caribbean Region, Elsa M. Chaney, 1985. US $5.00.

Report on the Condition of Central American Refugees and Migrants, Edelberto Torres-Rivas, 1985. US $5.00.

To order, add an additional $1.00 for postage and handling, for each publication. Make check payable to **GEORGETOWN UNIVERSITY**, Center for Immigration Policy and Refugee Assistance, Box 2298-- Hoya Station, Washington D.C. 20057 (202) 687-7032.

Notes

Notes